Volcano Man

Robin Holcomb as told to Darleen Ramos

Contents

Rigby
A Harcourt Achieve Imprint

www.Rigby.com
1-800-531-5015

Chapter 1:
My First Volcano
Eruption at Kilauea!

Can you imagine seeing a volcano blow up? I moved to the island of Hawaii because I wanted to study live volcanoes.

I saw my first volcano erupt on the night of September 24, 1971. I was in my house near the Hawaiian Volcano Observatory, or HVO, which was built so that people could study volcanoes. It is located on the edge of the Kilauea Volcano. The alarms went off when several small earthquakes happened one after another. I ran outside with the other scientists to see what was happening.

There was so much fog that it wasn't easy to see anything. I could hear the rocks making loud snapping, popping, and crackling sounds. They were breaking apart and falling into the cracks of a crater.

A Fiery Sky

Suddenly a red glow shot into the sky. Kilauea Volcano was erupting, and I was excited! A roaring sound came from the volcano, growing louder and louder.

It was the first time I had seen a volcanic eruption in person, and it was really beautiful! A wall of melted rock, called a "curtain of fire," spread across the floor of the caldera. (A caldera is a big hole, a few miles wide and hundreds of feet deep, which is formed when the top of a volcano caves in.)

Kilauea eruption of September 24, 1971

6:30 P.M.	A group of small earthquakes begins.
7:10 P.M.	HVO workers begin to arrive.
7:20 P.M.	Eruption begins on the caldera floor.
8:05 P.M.	Lava begins to flow across Crater Rim Road.
10:15 P.M.	Wall of lava has moved more than 1/2 mile.
4:00 A.M.	Eruptions stop, but begin again later.

Chapter 2:

Living on the Edge

Messages from Inside the Earth

As you can see, it is important for people who study volcanoes, called volcanologists, to learn what is happening under the earth's surface. They use tools to record earthquakes because earthquakes sometimes happen right before a volcanic eruption. Then scientists can warn the people who live nearby so that they can leave the area as soon as possible.

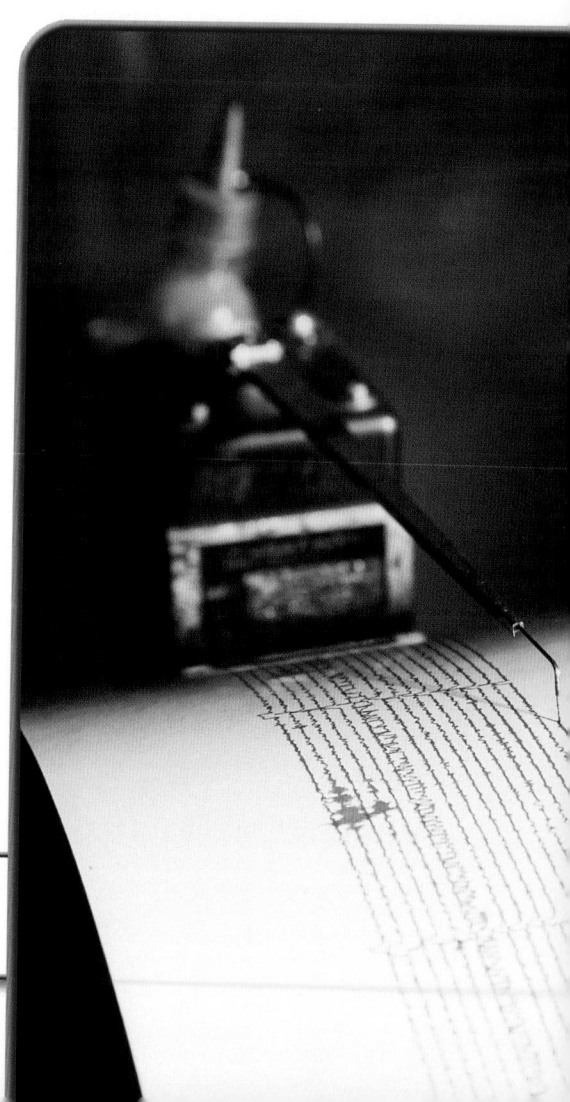

This is a machine that volcanologists use to record earthquakes.

Because I lived in a house near Kilauea Volcano, which is one of many volcanoes in Hawaii, I had to get used to living with earthquakes, too. When there are many small earthquakes in a row, that is a sign that a volcano is about to erupt. This is exactly what happened with Kilauea.

The strongest earthquake I personally ever experienced was

Volcanoes on the Island of Hawaii

Kohala
Mauna Kea
Hualalai
Mauna Loa
Kilauea

N
NW   NE
W   E
SW   SE
S

PACIFIC OCEAN

in 1975. My family and I woke up when we heard a loud thump and a crack. Our house was moving one way and then another! The earthquake was so strong that it moved furniture and made pictures and dishes fall on the floor.

Standing on Shaky Ground

Suddenly I heard a loud roar coming from the volcano. My small children were crying, so I tried to cross the hallway to get to their bedroom. The house was shaking so much that I couldn't stand up. Crawling across the floor, I finally reached their room. I had to put my hands against both sides of their doorway so that I could stand up.

Destruction

After the shaking stopped, we drove to HVO. On the main road, I saw that the earth had opened up and a car had fallen into it. Thankfully, the two people inside were safe. When we got to the observatory, the melted rock that was inside the Kilauea volcano suddenly shot up in the air. It was exciting to see.

This is Kilauea erupting after the earthquake.

The lava lake drained after the earthquake, leaving this empty crater.

That night we fixed equipment, studied the new eruption, and answered telephone calls from people who had been scared by the earthquake. At sunrise we learned that a troop of Boy Scouts had been camping at Halape Beach. The beach had been flooded by an enormous wave. It had carried the campers and some people who were fishing onto the big rocks. Luckily, the boys only suffered a few cuts and bruises.

This is Halape Beach, which was flooded by a large wave during the earthquake.

Chapter 3

Studying Volcanoes

What Do Volcanologists Do?

I became a volcanologist because I wanted to study volcanoes and find out how they work. Volcanologists must make many measurements before and after an eruption. They take pictures of eruptions, measure the sizes of earthquakes, and identify and measure the amount of gases the volcano produces.

I am using a machine that measures the temperature on the surface of a lava stream.

They also collect samples of melted rock. Some volcanologists study the melted rock to see what they can learn about what happens beneath Earth's surface.

This volcanologist is collecting a sample of hot lava.

What Is Lava?

A volcano erupts when magma, or hot melted rock from inside Earth, reaches Earth's surface. Because magma has gas in it, it can explode when it reaches the surface. You can think of magma as if it's soda in a soda bottle. When you shake a soda bottle and then open it, the soda sprays out. Magma does the same thing. When magma reaches the surface, it bursts out of the volcano. After magma comes out of the volcano, we call it lava. Lava can be as hot as 2,100° Fahrenheit.

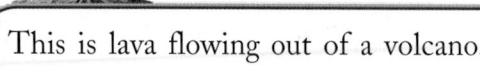
This is lava flowing out of a volcano.

Lava Lakes

One of my jobs at HVO was to take pictures of the erupting volcanoes, lava flows, and lava lakes. I would often go up to the edge of the lava lake at sunset and take photos of the purplish-black cooled lava around the lake. Sometimes I would go up to the edge of the lake in late afternoon and stay until late at night taking photos of the bursting bubbles and lake overflows in the darkness.

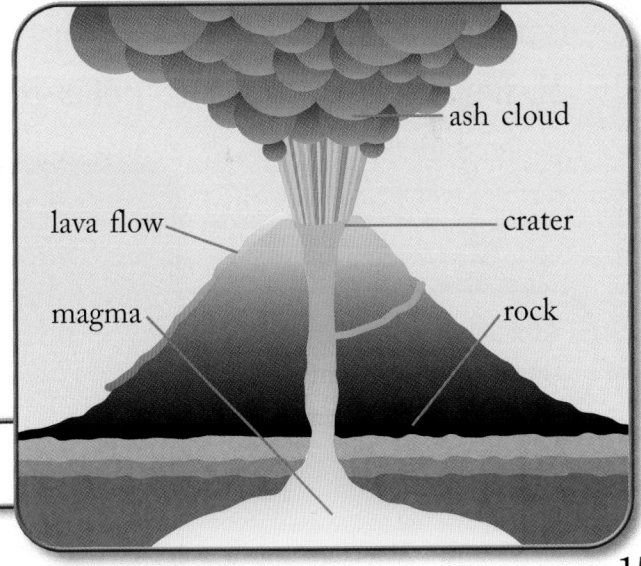

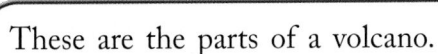

These are the parts of a volcano.

ash cloud

crater

lava flow

rock

magma

Mauna Loa

There are several other active volcanoes on Earth, but some are larger and more active than others. Mauna Loa, also in Hawaii, is the largest active volcano on Earth. Its name means long mountain. It doesn't erupt very often, but when it does, the eruption is huge. The scientists at HVO knew an eruption was coming, but we didn't know when. On July 5, 1975, the alarms rang in our houses because Mauna Loa was erupting after 25 years of silence. We couldn't believe it.

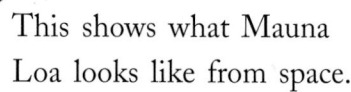

This shows what Mauna Loa looks like from space.

Are All Volcanoes in Hawaii?

Not all volcanoes are in Hawaii! Hawaii is just one state that has active volcanoes. Here are some other volcanoes that you might like to learn more about.

- Mount Hood in Oregon
- Mount Shasta in California
- Mount St. Helens in Washington
- Mount Rainier in Washington

This is Mount St. Helens in Washington.

I boarded a small airplane to view the eruption from above. I couldn't wait to take some great pictures. We flew up into the clouds until we finally saw a red glow. It was the biggest eruption I had ever seen! Clouds of volcanic smoke rose above the fire that was several miles long.

This shows the Mauna Loa volcano with a lot of smoke coming off the hot lava.

We saw beautiful trails of melted rock. The melted rock began to drop over the crater. It looked like a waterfall. But this was hot rock instead of water! The pilot tried to fly closer so that I could get better pictures, but the hot air made it unsafe.

Chapter 4:
All in a Day's Work
Dangerous Work

Working on an erupting volcano is risky, so it's necessary to wear boots to protect your feet. Not everyone who visits the volcano has on the right clothing and shoes. I was once taking a group of scientists up to the crater so that they could do some experiments.

This is what volcanic glass looks like.

Some young people saw us, and they decided to join us. This was a bad idea because they were wearing sandals. As they walked across sharp-edged pieces of volcanic glass, they cut their feet. I used my radio to call an ambulance, and we carried them out of the crater. Sometimes kindness is also a part of a volcanologist's job.

Under the Sea

Volcanic activity also takes place under the ocean. I was once lucky enough to be able to go deep into the ocean in a small submarine called ALVIN to see the cracks where the earth was splitting apart. It was a 2-hour trip down to the sea floor, but I was able to look out of a small 12-inch window all the way down.

Some of the cracks were less than a half-inch wide, but some of them were more than 3 feet wide! A few of the wide cracks were coated with glassy lava. I imagined that hot lava had flowed through them and then froze.

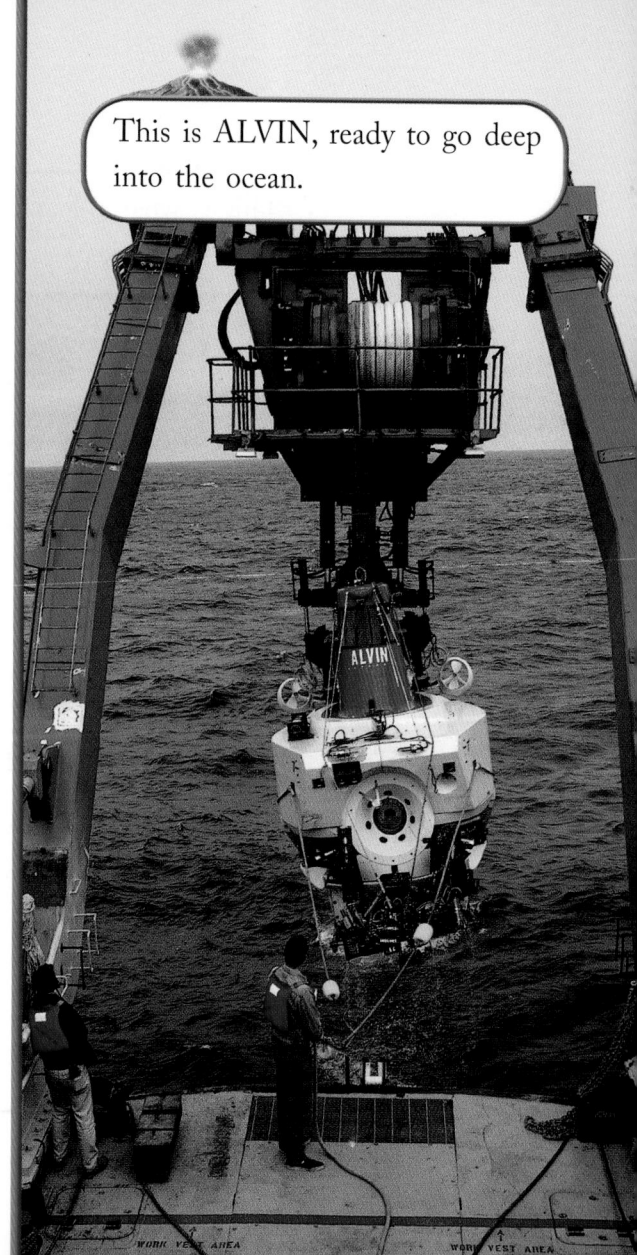

This is ALVIN, ready to go deep into the ocean.

ALVIN can go down to the sea floor to explore.

As a volcanologist, I get to study many exciting things both above and below the ground. Each day brings a new adventure and a new chance to help people. You never know what tomorrow may bring when you work with volcanoes!

Fun Facts

- ALVIN is owned by the United States Navy, and it has many tools for collecting things from under the ocean.
- One of the most famous dives ALVIN made was when it took scientists down to look at the *Titanic*, the famous ship that sank in 1912.

Index